Dear john,
The Diary
of a
Prostitute

By

Julia Anderson

Published by Julia Anderson
Distributed by Amazon

*****

TABLE OF CONTENTS

*****

PREFACE

The author of this book is a survivor of human trafficking and wrote the following pages directly from her experience. To protect the privacy and identity of others referenced in this book, names have either been changed or removed. Additionally, there remains a certain degree of safety risk in writing about some experiences or details and therefore those remain withheld.

*****

I'd like to acknowledge my mom, Paula, for her unconditional support in the four-plus years it took for me to birth this book, but more than that, she sat through readings listening to every brutal detail. These are things a mother should never have to hear about her daughter, let lone from her daughter and I am forever grateful.

INTRODUCTION

This is a collection of letters, written by a prostitute who came to find out that she was a victim of human trafficking. Each letter is addressed to a significant figure who impacted her journey through that time period. While the letters are all addressed Dear john, some may be reference a relationally different figure, which is made clear at the start of the letter. The only letters not following suit are last letter and the first one, parts of which were taken from an actual suicide note.

CHAPTER 1 - SOULMATE

Dear Soulmate,

I have never met you and I doubt I ever will, but I know you. I've known you all my life. Ever since I was a little girl, I've imagined my Prince Charming. I dreamed of what our life would be like together. But too much has happened over the course of my life that I'm sure that I won't survive long enough to see your face and even if I do, I'm too tarnished for you now...

My heart has been more than broken, more than shattered... it has been suffocated, deadened, poisoned, raped and tortured, confused and manipulated, and removed. All that's left is a dark empty space in the core of my chest. My blood runs cold and I remain emotionless; all that once passionately propelled me forward into my destiny has been ruthlessly stripped and stolen away from me.

My hopes and my dreams of knowing you, loving you, and sharing a life with you have slowly faded away with each encounter of evil demons disguised as family, friends, and 'normal everyday people'. I am too tainted for you now. You deserve someone pure, you deserve the someone I once was... the someone I never again will be.

I still think of you, often. You are so beautiful in my mind. You are strong and confident yet gentle and tender. Your compassion and your heart is, quite possibly, the one component that would be able to soften the hardness that has consumed me... if I were to embrace it. But, my darling, in all the years my heart - my soul - has known you and loved you, I know you deserve more than what I now am... and I couldn't let you settle for me.

To be alive and be this empty, to be so cold is lonely and leaves me struggling to understand the purpose... why I'm still here, with no hope of knowing joy, happiness, and love. I know I can't last like this much longer... but before I go, I wanted to write a letter to all the men who have impacted my life, who have made me who I am today... and my love, although I have never seen you with my eyes, I have seen you with my heart almost all my life.

We've danced, we've laughed, we've done so much together - in my dreams. The pursuit of finding you, of knowing you, had kept my hope alive of having a happy marriage in spite of the abusive, adulterous disaster of my parents'. Believing that you were real helped me to keep trying to escape the world of sex trafficking, a life of rape-for-profit, because deep in me I believed there was one good man out there somewhere.

As I write this, I'm not sure... but if you do exist, I am sure I will never have the chance to know you.

Perhaps, someday, long after I die, this diary will find it's way to you, and then you will have known me too.

With love,
Your other half

CHAPTER 2 - KIDNAPPED

Dear john,

So many emotions pour through me when I think of you. I think the strongest one is confusion. On one hand, I'm extremely glad you're dead... I don't have to run from you anymore. I don't have to constantly look over my shoulder wondering if you've found me or if you're going to take me again. But on the other hand, I'm very angry that you're dead. I think you got off way too easy. My kids and I still have to deal with all the pain and trauma you caused... and so do our loved ones as they deal with us and our issues. Yet there you are, dead. It's very ambivalent for me.

When I first met you, you seemed like a normal guy. I actually looked up to you and since you were more than twenty years older than me, I felt safe confiding in you as a mentor. I was only twenty-four, had just moved across the country with two kids and had started a new job of which I had no prior experience. You took me under your wing, helped me feel confident in my skills and taught me what I needed to know in order to do my job well. You helped get me an office set up in my home so I could be with my kids when they got out of school. I felt especially privileged when you took your own personal time after work to meet with me to discuss upcoming sales promos or go over the agenda for Monday's weekly conference call with the Corporate Office so that I was always well prepared. At my 30-day evaluation, when I was offered a promotion, I felt your investment in me played a big role... that salary meant a lot for me and my kids.

At work, we became a strong team and company sales were fast increasing. I was so proud of my performance and thankful to you for your mentorship. You showed interest in my kids when I brought them into the office. You said 'hi' if we ever saw you at the store or Starbucks or someplace out-and-about. You even offered a listening ear when I was frustrated with my ex-boyfriend who couldn't come to terms with the fact that our relationship was over and too depressed to get his act together and move out of my house.

I admit that I really didn't know you outside of work and you frequently made comments or gestures that didn't make sense to me, almost as if you were making a pass or an inappropriate joke. However, that just didn't make sense given the nature of our relationship, so I figured I must have just interpreted it wrong. I've been known to be naive or too literal anyway. I realize now that those were red flags I should have paid attention to. Honestly, though, at the time I had no idea that you were simply grooming me and setting me up right from the start.

After about three months of being 'nice', your behavior changed. There was one night when we were at the office late. You ordered pizza for the sales team to motivate them to hit their goal. You had me go pick it up and then invited me to eat in the back office with you, alone, for a 'working' dinner. You commented on my figure (I had recently lost a little weight) and you gazed way too long... I felt so uncomfortable. Do you remember? After a few slices, I got up to leave, but you backed me up against the wall as if you were going to kiss me or touch me. I said don't. You didn't. You just stood there over me, about an inch away from my face. I could feel your breath on me as you stared coldly into my eyes. I was really scared, john, and you knew it.

Not long after that night, you asked me to dinner. Initially, I declined, the pizza incident still fresh in my mind. You were persistent and apologetic and really just wanted to make it up to me. Naive as I was, I gave in, agreeing to go for a quick bite. When you pulled into my driveway to drop me off after dinner, you said it would really piss off my ex if we stayed in the car for a few minutes. It would make him think that we were on a date which would help motivate him to 'move on'. I didn't think that was such a good idea, plus I wanted to get inside to kiss my kids good-night. You insisted and once again had that same ice-cold demeanor about you that scared me enough not to move. A few minutes passed by as you played AC/DC and then with a very rushed "thank you very much, good night" I hurried out of the car and into my house. I didn't realize how unsafe I had felt until I was safe inside... and it didn't make any sense to me.

Shortly after that, we had a working dinner that had already been planned at a restaurant close to work. My intentions were to hurry through and get home quickly, but you made sure that didn't happen. I remember having a glass of wine with dinner... Then I remember being in a dream, in an apartment I'd never seen before. You snorted cocaine up your nose so I KNEW it was a dream... but it was kind of funny that I dreamt that because I've never been around drugs my whole life.. I wouldn't have known that. There was music I've never heard before playing in my dream..it gave me a headache. That's all I dreamt. Except I woke up groggy the next morning with just my underwear on in YOUR bed! I started thinking it wasn't a dream. I assume you slipped something into my drink at the restaurant the night before. I felt violated and so betrayed. You were someone I trusted, someone I looked up to. I demanded to know what happened yet you simply said to calm down. You said I had way to much to drink at the restaurant, you didn't think my kids should see me that way so you let me sleep it off at your place. When I asked why you took off my clothes... you sternly said that I did.

I didn't know what to believe. You had this way of being both wrong and right at the same time and I was powerless to prove either one. I was angry at you, and made sure you knew it, for not taking me home regardless of how drunk you thought I was. The only bed I belonged in each and every night was my own! You let me be upset... I guess it was worth it because you had set all your pieces up perfectly.

A week later, out of no where, the business owner, our boss, took me to lunch to let me know that they just found out some information about you and to give me a heads-up. She told me you're a convicted felon and registered sex offender, one of the offenses against A MINOR, and that you're recently released from prison. Your rap sheet was a mile long and you've been in and out of prison for more than half your life! They fired you that day. I was told I had to make a decision: either I kept my relationship with you or kept my job. WHAT?! I reassured her I had no relationship with you what-so-ever. She wasn't so easily convinced, asking about private office meetings, flirtations in the workplace, dinner dates, and sleepovers... and that you frequently referred to us as dating. I was shocked! I tried to explain how I was set up and that, again... there is NO relationship of any kind. She conceded and I kept my job. I left that lunch feeling confused, betrayed and again, violated. I was so thankful I would never have to see you or deal with you again; But it wasn't over.

You showed up at my house later that day. I wouldn't let you in. You came in anyway. You choked me, slammed my head into the floor, backed me into he corner of the shower and TOLD me that your apartment and car were being confiscated (as they were a part of your salary), that you were living with me now and that I was going to do exactly what you told me from that point forward. I tried to tell you what happened at lunch... that I knew about you and your past. You chose that moment, with your hands tightly around my neck, to share with me the details of your past that aren't on record... just to make certain I knew what you were capable of.

Do you have any idea what was going through my mind? My kids would be home from school soon, I had no idea if you would hurt them. I knew the things you had been accused of and the things you had been convicted of. I knew most of your crimes involved violence against women and children. I was scared you would hurt or kill me... and then what would happen to my kids? I remember this was the first time you physically hurt me (that I was conscious for). I also knew it wouldn't be the last. After that, it went black.

You beat and strangled me almost every day for the next several weeks. You told my kids you were their new dad... they were petrified! They weren't even allowed to talk to me without your permission. No one could move, go to the bathroom, get a glass of water, wake up, go to sleep, anything without asking you first. It was pure mental and physical torture.

Thankfully, you didn't lay a hand on my kids... at least not yet. Within just a few weeks you had all my money - thousands of dollars - and you had decided I would be your wife. You had laid out a black dress and had for me black roses, you said it was much like my funeral, I was marrying the devil, after-all. It was a very dark day - the beginning of my ending.

I think the only thing I was happy about was the fact that your penis was broken. You never could make it work, and for that I was so thankful. But that didn't stop you... You would rape me with anything within your reach... knives, wood, sharp plastic... you would hurt me until I passed out. But for me, I was thankful you didn't get the satisfaction of doing it yourself. Instead, I had the satisfaction of knowing that your manhood was perpetually and eternally frustrated... no matter how bad you hurt me.

Soon after my ending had begun, you packed us up and set us on the road across the country, strategically placing my six-year old son with you in your car and my seven-year old daughter with me in mine pulling the trailer. I couldn't make a run for it because you had my son and you had all my money. At every stop I tried to see how he was doing, but he wouldn't speak. Each night, you beat me in the bathroom of the motels. You beat me for crazy reasons. Once, it was because in Mississippi it rained so hard you couldn't see. Apparently it was my fault we didn't make it to the motel in time to miss the rain storm. Another time it was because the pizza delivery didn't come in 30 minutes or less. I never knew which way was up. There seemed to be no way to guarantee my safety. You were a ticking time bomb and I had no idea what would set you off.

Once we got to our destination, you forced me to use my identity to start a business (you being a convicted criminal, yours was no good) and you put my kids and I to work 15-20 hours a day. We lived out of a motel for nearly 6 months while remodeling an office which you quickly turned into a boiler room, scamming people over the phone. You did finally move us from the motel to a house in a very quiet neighborhood, which actually made things worse.

Let me sum this up: you began to use my children to force me to commit criminal activity on your behalf by beating them with belts, bashing my daughter's head open on a sink, beating her face until it swelled up like an alien, starving them, forcing them to clean toilets and polish silverware 10-12 hours a day, threaten to drop them off in the wilderness when I was unconscious... this list goes on.

You had began force-feeding me drugs, you forced me to get a breast augmentation and then you beat me when you brought me home from surgery, rupturing an incision, so I had to go back for a second surgery. You never let me sleep. If I ever fell asleep, you would strangle me awake and as I woke up gasping for air I would see you over me, smiling, saying "good morning sunshine". I never had any idea what day it was.

The only time you let me leave the house was to run an errand for you, but you kept one or both my children and you gave me a specific task with a time limit, told me exactly how many miles I was allowed to put on the car and I was to bring back exactly the change that was indicated on the receipt along with a threat of what would happen to the kids if I defaulted on any one of these items in addition to my own punishment.

I think your favorite thing to do though was to make me think I was crazy. You would assign chores for the day, like putting away the folded clothes that were in a pile on the bed. It's a chore I've done for you numerous times before and you've taught me, by way of countless beatings, how you like your drawers organized: black socks with black, white with white, etc.I know to report to you once I'm finished and move on to the next item on my very long list.

About 35-40 minutes later, you would come storming in, grab me by my hair and drag me down the hall into the bedroom. Pointing at the clothes, you'd yell "I told you to put the clothes away!"

"I did!" I would cry. But there on the bed, neatly stacked were the pile of clothes. I was SURE I just put those away... but I couldn't argue with the fact that they were, in fact, right in front of my eyes. You beat me badly and left me to complete my chore. You were so smug.

Damaged, confused, and bleeding, I again put the clothes away, double checked that I really did do it, and went back to you to report for my next chore. You stormed in 35 minutes later dragging me by my hair back to the bedroom again, screaming so loud the windows were shaking "I TOLD you to put the clothes away! What is the MATTER with you?!?! You wanna get beat??" Do you remember john...? I said nothing. I saw the pile of clothes neatly stacked on the bed as if they had never been touched. You had me so confused. I really thought I had put them away... twice... but here you were yelling at me and the clothes were on the bed... you beat me again, more severely than the first time, and left me to complete my assignment.

Again, 35 minutes later, you were dragging me by my hair back into the bedroom for a THIRD time, calling me terrible names, demanding to know why I was such a bitch who didn't know how to simply put a few clothes away. You did this the WHOLE day. You did this with me, you did this with my kids. I had bald spots on my head where huge chucks of hair was missing from where you ripped it out from dragging me back and forth all day...it took months to grow back to where I could get it cut so it didn't look abnormal. This is how you broke my will.

When I tell people about this, some of them call this domestic abuse. Let me be clear with you, john: there was NOTHING domestic about this. We were not a couple. In spite of your ridiculous wedding ceremony, I was NEVER your wife. You may have a marriage certificate, but I did NOT consent to that. You FORCED my 'I do'. You kidnapped me and my children. You took me against my will. You threatened me, used violence, and drugged me from the very beginning of this whole situation. You force me (and my children) into involuntary servitude. You forced us to work at your office day, after day, after day... No food, no rest, no choice. I know your history with prostitution and I know what you were setting up in that house before you got busted. I now know where this was going.

I have spent a lot of years feeling guilty because I thought this was my fault. I thought maybe I did something to cause this to happen... or maybe because I thought you were nice and trusted you in the beginning that I brought this on myself and therefore should have done something to get myself out.

However, after over a decade of craziness and just as much therapy, I've learned that this is YOUR fault and YOUR responsibility. You did this. You caused this. You are the criminal and I'm done owning all or part of what you've done.

Thankfully, you couldn't keep up this charade within the community. Eventually, someone got suspicious and my daughter courageously spoke up. I'll never forget the way this went down and because of this letter, neither will you.

The night before, after you nearly beat me senseless, you made me stay up all night transferring all your 'business data' to a different database. Violence in the house had escalated to knives, burns, and guns. I worked hard. I finished just in time to get ready to leave for the 'office'. You had hired a nanny, which was our blessing and your biggest mistake. Your ego got in the way. I guess you just can't control everybody... and you couldn't control her.

She saw my wounded face, but I assured her that it was my clumsiness that caused the black eyes and other bruising and strangulation marks... she politely pretended that I was convincing. I kissed my kids goodbye, I was thankful that they finally didn't have to be at the 'office' anymore. You, on the other hand, barked harsh orders of 500 jumping jacks per kid, toilets to be done, and a whole list of other things. I stood behind you looking at the nanny, rolling my eyes.

We left and you yelled the whole way. An hour after we got to the 'office', the police called telling me to come home. You sent me to the house alone. When I got there, no one was there. Just one cop. He would not tell me where my kids were. He didn't offer me safety. He didn't asked about my visible injuries. He only asked me if I was in any danger.

That was my chance right there, john. I blew it. That was my chance. I was so scared of you. You had me convinced that you could find me ANYWHERE. You had me believing that because you had been in and out of the prison system all across the country for more than half your life, that you were owed favors and that half of them were from the "good guys".

The cop again asked me if I was in danger, I froze. I'm not allowed to answer this question, so I said "I don't know." He gave me his card and said if I figure it out, to give him a call. Then he left. That was it. You started blowing up my phone demanding to know where I was and for me to get back. I wanted to run. But, I knew you'd find me. I had no money. I had already asked my mom for help. She couldn't. I had asked my dad for help. He wouldn't.

I had no where to go, no money. I didn't know where my kids were. I had no idea when I would see them again. ...And then I had you telling me I was your property. You owned me. I didn't know how to get away from you.

I knew I needed to figure that out. I went back to the office.

You beat me for three days straight. I was unconscious for most of it. You were arrested. I was arrested. You were charged. Child abuse. As for me, they again were trying to give me an opportunity to make a statement against you. I didn't. I was petrified. I told them there was nothing I could say although the marks you left on my body were visible. Apparently that's not enough for the cops. I was charged, although later they were dropped. You bailed yourself out... you bailed me out. I begged them not to release me to you, but well, they did.

I thought life was hell in the months up to this point... but as it turned out, these next few months gave hell a whole new meaning. You regularly behaved as though you believed you were actually the devil and the marks I still carry on my body hold those memories. You branded me as your property with your name and date and some other information, which I have had removed and covered up. The beatings were a cakewalk compared to the torture you were now putting me through... it is the things you did to me during these months that I have still not been able to speak of or even write down.

Honestly, john, it really hurts me so much that you have done things to me that I can't even say out loud... not even if I'm by myself. I can say that to you now, because there's nothing you can do to me anymore. I can be vulnerable and I can have a soft heart and I can feel my feelings because you can't hurt me with it.

Finally, that torture was over and you were put away.

For a few months, I was a zombie. I didn't know what to do... you had controlled my every move, I didn't know how to think for myself. I was still scared that if I made a wrong move, somehow you'd know and I would be punished. For the first little while, I even came to see you in jail out of sheer terror that you had people hunting me.

Eventually, though, I gained a little bit of courage, and a little more, and a little more. One day, I decided not to answer your collect call. Then, I moved away from the house of hell. It had been months; I still hadn't seen my kids; I still didn't know where they were… This mother's heart dying more every day. But, no matter where I moved, you found me. I would get a letter from you... or a phone call. You wouldn't let me go. You threatened me. You reminded me I belonged to you and that you would come get what was yours.

You said if you can't have me, no one could have me. I ended up working for a pimp, by accident, all because I was trying to hide from you.

Less than a year later, you got out! Deeper underground I went. The life I was forced to live by the very nature of your existence is indescribable... You stole my life.

I changed my identity more than 8 times trying to hide from you. I don't even know how many other pimps I worked for trying to stay hidden from you. I stayed away from my kids trying to stay alive and keep them safe from you. You stole my motherhood. I have tried to kill myself because being dead would be better than being alive with you. I lost my soul trying to lose you. I truly died trying to survive you.

I spent the better part of 8 years running from you - it became my first priority, my career. Staying steps ahead of you was what I was best at, knowing where you were before you knew where I was... I mastered my skill-set. When I found out all those years later that you finally died, I went into shock. I celebrated for one night. That was it.

I spent the next two years lost and confused. I didn't know how to live free. You had dominated an entire decade. In one way or another, my life revolved around you. Now... it was over. My skill-set was no longer needed. I had nothing to run from.

For the first time in my life, I could start thinking about what I wanted. This is why I write to you, john. Because, now that I finally had the opportunity to live for myself, so much has happened that I almost didn't think that I could. For several years after your death, I found myself stuck in a world I didn't know how to get out of because that's all I knew... that's what YOU trained me for.

'Happy' scared me. 'Free' scared me more. I didn't know how to be a Person. It was only a few years ago that I found out that what you did to us is called Human Trafficking. To be specific, john... you forced me and my kids into labor trafficking by working for you, not getting paid, not being free to leave, working under the threat of and actual violence; you forced us into involuntary servitude by the same standards. I'm the victim of forced marriage. You took away my personhood and turned me into a possession, nothing more than a product to be used, sold or purchased, or thrown away. You programmed me in a way that cannot be undone - much like an abused dog will forever cower at a sudden movement, I too will always instinctually think 'product' first, 'person' second.

You, by far, single-handedly caused more damage than any other person I have ever encountered. At the time of your death, I was still waiting to be re-united with my kids. It had been 10 years. You stole them from me. You caused that. The only way I could survive that was to turn off my heart. I turned it off from everybody. I had become cold and ruthless...passionless. I wasn't sure I could ever turn it back on. You have shown me more pure evil than most people could have nightmares about.

I don't know why you are the way you are, john. I don't know if something happened to you in your childhood...

or if there is a mis-fire in your brain. People ask me all the time why you did what you did. I think that is the stupidest question in the world. I have no idea why. But, here's what I do know:

I know that I have survived you. I know that my kids will be ok. I know that we will be able to work through the wreckage you left inside us and each of us will touch the world in a very special and unique way because of you. I know that you have done the worst to me, but you never got the best of me. Most importantly, I know you didn't win... I am free now and my heart can love again.

CHAPTER 3 - AND I BECAME

Dear john,

You were my first, but not my last. I find it ironic as I look back on our time together that you were the only one who knew what to expect from our encounter. Usually, it's the other way around. I don't think you realize how much impact you had on me... not just as a person, but also in my career.

We met in Vegas at the Monte Carlo. You knew me as Ruby and you were my very first call. I was running from a very dangerous man and trying to lay low. I needed money to live, but I couldn't risk being 'on the grid' so I looked for jobs that paid cash. I found an ad for DANCERS & MODELS - NO EXPERIENCE NEEDED and applied. This back-alley agency offered me a job as a private dancer. I had never done anything like that before, but I was a dancer growing up (tap, jazz, ballet...) so I thought it couldn't be that different. The lady who hired me at the agency told me it was pretty much the same and that I wouldn't have to do anything I wasn't comfortable with. Rather than dancing in front of a crowd, we did private performances. It's Vegas. As far as pay, the agency charged a fee which I collect and drop 100% of it back at the agency. I get to keep tips only. I was fine with that, money was money. She also was very careful to articulate that prostitution is illegal in Las Vegas.

I wasn't really sure why she was telling me that, but I've been down on the strip and that sort of thing happened a lot there, so my guess was that they were just covering all the bases. I was so unsure about doing that, john, but I needed to make money so badly. You didn't know my situation, but I needed to stay safe and get back to my kids... I decided to suck it up and make the best of it.

I put together a few sexy outfits and some music I knew I could really move to, I felt I was ready to 'entertain'. At 4am I got the call to come to your room. I was nervous and shaking the whole drive there. I've never danced for just one person before unless I was being cast for a part in a show - but that's different. When I got to your door, I got a call from the agency saying that for my safety, they'll stay on the phone with me while I collect the fee.

I was curious how they knew I was even at your door.

Anyway, as you recall, you paid me the $200 agency fee and then they told me to call back when I was done. For me, so far, so good. But then you started asking about the menu. Remember? You were so frustrated with me because you wanted to know what was on the menu and I kept saying 'I don't know, I've never eaten there before.'

You thought I was being a smart ass. Well, I wasn't. I honestly thought you were hungry. I had no idea you were asking about sex. I had no idea I was there to have sex with you or perform sexual favors. So when I asked what you were in the mood for... and you said everything.. I was thinking WOW he's really hungry! So I said "Go ahead, get everything!"

Then you asked me how much it would be for everything. That's when I got irritated. I'm not a walking price list. I asked "How much is it normally?" You must have got frustrated too, because you set down $500 on the night stand and came back to me and proceeded to take your 'everything'.

I should tell you that I never gave you my consent. I had thought you were talking about food.

You should also know that I've been raped before, more than once, more than twice. So, when you came over and began to touch me and take off my clothes, the fact that I was frozen also was not my consent. It was fear. I couldn't move, I couldn't speak, I couldn't say no because I was paralyzed by fear - fear from past trauma, fear from present trauma happening at that very moment.

This situation was brand new. I had no concept for what was happening. On the surface, it appeared that I was there by my own free will and was participating consensually (in illegal and unethical behavior, by the way). But truthfully, I felt deceived. I was not given full disclosure as to what might happen upon my arrival. I realize this makes me naive. Fine. That doesn't excuse what happened, which is non-consensual sex - otherwise known as rape.

I realize that from your perspective, it wasn't rape. You paid a $200 agency fee plus an additional $500 to have sex with Ruby. You got what you paid for. You had no idea that I didn't know what I was doing or why I was there or that I didn't want to be there. I don't know what kind of guy you are, or if any of that information would have made a difference to you.

But, here's what happened after I left. I went home and stayed in my shower for THREE days. I didn't eat. I didn't leave the shower for three days. I drank water from the faucet if I was thirsty. I was so ashamed with what had happened and what I had done... I kept trying to wash it off. When the water ran cold I turned it off until the water got hot again. I cried until I ran out of tears and when they came back, I cried some more.

I somehow had just become a prostitute.

I didn't intend for that to happen... but I couldn't undo it. Where was I supposed to go from here? Can you imagine, john, your sister or your daughter in this situation? In a bad situation in life, she makes a bad decision and ends up here. What would you tell her? What would you want for her at this point?

Would you hold her and tell her it's over and that it's going to be ok? Or would you tell her that she's stuck with that label and she better get used to being a hooker?

Unfortunately, I didn't have anyone to hold me or tell me it was going to be ok. All I had was you telling me to take my money and leave, as you lit a cigarette when you were finished with me. I suppose you were one of the luckier ones... since you got me at the beginning of my career, when I was fresh. How were you to know you would be the first of thousands that I would be sold to? Since you, I've hosted 11 years worth of men like you. My question is would you want that for you sister or your daughter or your wife?

If you were less concerned with having sex with a strange girl who really wasn't named Ruby and you were more concerned with being a person, you might have noticed that I was nervous. You may have picked up on the fact that I didn't know what you were talking about. You may have paused long enough to talk to me as a fellow human being and as a result, our encounter could have ended with an honorable exchange. You could have had the opportunity to empower me rather than exploit me.

Thankfully today, I finally recognize that I'm worth way more than $700. I'm worth one man for one lifetime.

CHAPTER 4 - THE ROYAL TREATMENT

Dear john,

When I met you at Caesar's Palace, I thought this would be the easiest money I would ever make. It was... and it wasn't.

I was still using the name 'Ruby' and had been a 'working girl' for only a few months, but in this gig you gotta learn fast to survive. I had learned a lot and experienced even more. I was a scared single mom, running for her life, doing whatever it took to stay alive and find a way back to her kids. I did everything I was told... and I was told to entertain you. All I knew about you was that you were some kind of royalty from over-seas, that you were a regular, and you had pre-paid for me for five hours. I was told that the other girls always enjoyed themselves and sometimes you'd extend their time.

When I first arrived, it felt like a vacation. You were in this humungous suite with several rooms and a butler's entrance. I was very impressed. Once you showed me around, you left me with your butler and said you'd be back later, that you had some business to take care of. While I found that odd, the butler reassured me all was well and brought me to a beautiful room with a fresh assortment of fruit and champagne waiting. He drew me a bath in the next room and said that my masseuse would be up in 30 minutes. I was to relax and enjoy myself, courtesy of you, john.

Two hours had passed already and I still hadn't done a single thing, but I was very relaxed, the champagne flowing and the masseur's hands melted me like butter. This truly was the easiest money I had made so far! It was about this time that you came in to check on me and smiled, appearing pleased that I was enjoying myself. Now you were ready for me, but even all that preparation didn't ready me for what was to come next.

You pre-paid me directly, very handsomely, and made sure to discuss what activities were allowed, what you really wanted and what was off limits. You had said you really enjoyed touching me and we made sure I was compensated for that. You made it clear that the money you were giving me was mine, not my pimp's - that he'd already been well compensated for my time.

When we got started, you went immediately between my legs with your fingers and it felt very unusual... tingly - not in a good way. I asked you what you were doing and why it was different. You didn't answer right away. You just kept sush-ing me. After about 15 minutes, my head started feeling fuzzy and my whole body was feeling weird. I tried to squirm away and finally you quietly whispered in my ear that you were inserting cocaine into my vagina.

I had been drugged against my will before... but never like this. The drugs I had been given before were to make me sleepy and groggy. You handed me a whole new situation - I had never been so high!

Can I just ask you... what makes you think it's ok to get someone high without their consent? You put so much cocaine inside me that before long, I wasn't able to make any kind of judgement about anything.

All I know is that three days later I came down.

I was with you for three whole days. I don't remember any of it. I assume you had me call my pimp to say I was done, otherwise he would have been looking for me. You bought me clothes (I know this because I was wearing them). I know we went to the Red Light Swingers Club because there was a stamp on my hand. What the hell happened there? Among the articles of clothes you bought me was an extremely large dildo... no wonder I was hurting and very sore. I do remember you had your driver drive me home, so thank you for that. You paid me well. But let me say that no amount of money is worth what you did to me.

I have no idea how many people I was with during that time. I don't know where we went or anything that I did. None of what happened is ok. I was raped. Raped by you and anyone else who you gave access to me. You used me and violated me by incapacitating my mind and my ability to choose.

What I am trying to say is that I am not a toy. No person is a toy. Even if you buy a person or pay for a person, it does not give you the right to do with them whatever you feel like doing. Their human rights are not suddenly null and void simply because you purchased them for sex. I don't care if you ARE royalty.

More than that, what does that say about you and anyone else who participated in those three days? Why do you have to drug a girl in order to have a good time with her? Is there no sober girl willing to enjoy your company?

I don't mean any disrespect, Your Highness, but I encourage you to deal with whatever issue that is inside your heart that you don't feel that you're worth genuine companionship with a woman. I'm sure that if you're honest, it was not your intent to cause harm to me or anyone else... and if you allow yourself to truly look at what happened, that's exactly what you did. You caused harm to me.

Do you realize that whenever I looked at those clothes (which are long since in the garbage) or drove past Caesars Palace or had any thoughts of you that I feel disgusted with myself? I can't erase what happened. What's worse, john, is that you started an addiction to cocaine for me. I was so high for those three days you didn't want me to crash hard, so you gave me enough to come down gradually. That was enough to start my habit.

Today, right now, I do take full responsibility for all my drug and alcohol use over the course of my life... and I also take full credit for getting clean. But you are responsible for introducing it into my body. You are responsible for drugging me against my will. I never asked for cocaine or even thought of doing it before you. My experience with you taught me something: that it was easier to 'prostitute' when I was high than when I was sober.

Before you, I thought there might still be a way out of this mess I was in. After you, I found myself in a viscous circle: the drugs just so I could deal with being a hooker and pay my pimp, using my pimp so I could stay hidden and safe from the guy who was trying to kill me, hooking enough to make extra cash for the drugs... round and round I go.

This was the end of Ruby.

After several missteps, I ended up working for a more elite operation that dealt strictly with high-end clientele. I now worked under the name Mona. I must have given you my number back during our session because I was shocked to get your phone call nearly a year later, requesting a session. After thinking it over, I accepted. I was no longer the sweet, naïve, innocent girl you once knew and I was not intimidated this time around.

I decided to offer you a special treat, so I brought a friend along with me... I don't know if you remember this or not... I'm guessing not. She and I did lines with you for about a half a day (although you were too high to notice that we didn't Actually inhale) and then we began to slip pills in your drinks to knock you out. Finally, you passed out.

Once we were sure that you'd be out for a bit, we went through your things and took about half of your casino chips - about $15,000. We left for most of the day and came back before you were fully awake. Then we all finished having 'fun', you paid us for our time and we left. You had no idea what we had done. After all was said and done, we walked away with $20,000 total. You called me later and asked me if I knew what you did most of the day because you were missing some chips. I told you that you insisted on going downstairs to gamble.

To this day, you thought you gambled it away. I used my ten grand to buy a car, cash out. My point being... it doesn't feel so good to be taken advantage of, does it?

CHAPTER 5 - ARE YOU MY FATHER?

Dear john,

There are many things we could talk about that have occurred over the course of our knowing each other, but what I want to discuss today has probably singularly had more impact on me than any other experience that you and I share.

Before I go on, I should tell you that even as I write this now, it is with a heavy heart and tear-filled eyes. There will always be a hole in my heart where you belong, because you're my dad. I don't know what it means to have a dad... and I believe this is the reason why:

The man who had taken me and my kids had had us for several months... I can't remember exactly how long, I've suffered too many head injuries (from all the beatings I've endured), so my memory can be a little foggy. I remember I had been scrounging, for a long time, spare change trying to save up to make a phone call. You see, dad, he would sometimes send me to the store. I was required to bring back exactly the amount of change indicated on the receipt...but I always looked on the street for money. If I found some, I'd take it back and hide it.

.

I finally had enough to make a phone call from a pay phone and so I waited for the next opportunity when he sent me to the store. I had given a lot of thought as to who I should make my ONE phone call to. I could call my mom and while she would want to help, she wouldn't be able to financially. I could call my grandma, but she wouldn't understand what I was saying and I didn't have time to try to explain it to her...we needed immediate help now.

I decided to call you. You were able to help us. You had an airplane, so you could come get us. You're a pilot for an airline, so you could just put us on a plane. You could afford to simply get us someplace safe.

The day finally came where I was sent to the store and I was so petrified that somehow he would find out I was making this phone call. But I had to try... I had to do something! He had been hurting my kids...and me...for so long. He was threatening to kill them, or me, or all of us. I didn't have many options, but this was one risk I had to take.

I made the call. You answered.

In hysterical tears, I explained what had happened, what was going on, that this was life or death and that we needed help. Do you remember what you said, dad? I do.

"I'm sorry Julia. I can't get involved with any negative Karma right now. There's nothing I can do."

... ...

Even now, I don't know what to say to that.

No, wait, yes I do. HELP YOUR KIDS. No matter what. ALWAYS help your kids.

I realize there's a lot of history in our family. You and mom had a really long, nasty divorce, there was abuse, violence, accusations thrown every which way. You and I have a long history and we each have very different versions, I understand that. But I'm still your daughter. I was still in danger. I needed your help. Your grandchildren needed your help! This was life or death. There is no reason on this earth, no possible reason what-so-ever, to not help your kids get out of danger.

So, let me explain what I had to do to protect myself: After assuming 8 different identities over the course of 8 years, I had to fake my own death and get a completely new identity. I had to stay away from my kids for over a decade to keep us all safe. I had to go from one pimp to another to stay protected from the dangerous man who kept finding me, which means I spent 11 years in the sex trade. You see, dad, our lives continued to be jeopardy until he finally died 10 years later. It wasn't just that one moment.

Is that the life you envisioned for your daughter? Was your 'Karma' worth it?

Yes, I'm angry. I've really tried to get over this one particular situation, but you had an opportunity to be my dad and save me from ALL of that. I don't blame you for what's happened in my life, my life is my life. But I do hold you responsible for the choices you make... and I hold you responsible for how those choices affect people.

Being a dad is a very big deal. It's a very important role to play in a person's entire life. (So is a mom...I'm still hoping to have that chance back in my own children's lives). I was only 24 years old with a 6 and 7 year old. I was in grave danger and I needed my dad. You don't say no in a situation like that. You do whatever it takes to get your kid(s) safe and you ask questions later.

But, you made your choice and I was forced to survive in a world of sex, drugs, and slavery. You and I don't talk.

I wish you made a different choice... You and I could have a relationship, and I would know what it means to have a father.

*****

CHAPTER 6 – THE MEN IN BLUE

Dear john,

When you raided the house, took my children and called me to come home, I was hoping you would take me too. When you asked me if I was in danger, I was scared. I was hoping you'd simply know that I was. Didn't you look at my face? Aren't you trained to observe? But you didn't notice the bruises and welts or you just didn't care. So, instead, I fearfully answered "I don't know" and you left me to 'figure it out'. My encounter with you only reiterated the message that my trafficker had been telling me: that the 'good guys' really were on his side. Were you?

Do you have any idea the baseline standard you set in that moment? I can't come to you for help. You're either not qualified to notice the obvious or you are too judgmental to care. I was technically the wife of a very bad man who was doing very terrible things to the children you just rescued. Thank you, by the way. But what makes you think your job was done?

When I was arrested side-by-side with my trafficker, as if I were partnered with him in some way, I was further victimized and everything that my trafficker had told me about the system just came true. Law enforcement can't be trusted. Government services can't be trusted. Three days had passed between the raid and the arrest of which the entire time he beat me senseless to ensure I wouldn't talk. He convinced me that if I said one single word about anything to anyone or disobeyed him in any way, he would kill me and my children would grow up motherless. Since he took us hostage, he had followed through with every threat he'd ever made with the one exception of death (although he did play Russian roulette with a gun to my head, so there's that). Unfortunately, I trusted him to keep his word, now, more than I trusted you to keep yours.

I'm just wondering though, at what point do you think you will be able to step in on a victim's behalf? How bad does it need to be? Even 24-48 hours of relief would have helped me. A shower. Food. SLEEP. Some time for the drugs to wear off, to think straight. If I could have seen that I could be safe for a little bit of time, I might have been able to establish some trust to share with you what was really going on and how much danger I was in.

But instead, what I understand is that I should have gone to the police if I needed help. So tell me... Just how is a prisoner supposed to advocate for herself?

Many years later, I found that the irony ran much deeper. I was told you were a regular so I wasn't worried about you being law enforcement... for me this would be business as usual. I greeted you at the door of a very upscale incall location to which you smiled a quick hi and you went straight into the shower and shut the door. Interesting start, I thought, but ok.

About eight minutes later, you emerged with only a towel around your waist. I tried to make brief conversation, but you kept quiet, looking at the bed, then out the window, then at the bed again.

Finally you asked "how much to go twice?" I quoted you the price, required it upfront and doubted you'd pull it off. You set the cash on the nightstand, dropped your towel and laid on the bed. Not in a sexy way... you just laid there.

Honestly, I felt awkward about the way this was progressing... not uncomfortable, just awkward. So, I undressed and laid next to you on the bed. Without saying a word you mounted me like a caveman and got yours... twice. Then you got up and headed back to the shower.

That's when I saw who your badge. I went in to another bathroom to get cleaned up and by the time I came out, you were gone. No thank you, no good-bye, nothing.
I was nervous at first wondering why you left so quickly. Then I wondered if I had done something wrong...I was so confused. Then I realized it was because of who you were.

You said one sentence to me the entire time... one sentence.

You saw me again often, about one or twice a week actually and all you said each time was "once" or "twice". That was it.

Let me ask you something, Officer, I know you saw me often, but did you ever actually see me? I'm wondering if you realized I'm a human, a person, a woman. Aren't you a cop? Isn't it your JOB to take care of people...not to exploit them? You didn't even see me, let alone treat me like a person. I was invisible to you. That bothers me. How am I supposed to rely on the police department for help when my total value is nothing more than a human blow up doll.

Why can't you see the situation I'm in? Aren't you educated? Aren't you aware that I'm trapped? Are you at least aware that prostitution is against the very law you're supposed to uphold? Is it ok to have a slave perform services for your selfish pleasure? Are you aware that you just purchased a human being? YOU just determined my total worth. How does that feel, Officer?

I can say that in my survivorship, my standards and my personal value far exceeds any badge that you may hold. Not only have I climbed out from the grips of traffickers', but I've climbed out of the deceit of yours. As a victim of a crime, I held hope for justice... for law to prevail over the perpetrators. Except you blur the blue line when you make justice the very violation.

But wait, it goes deeper. The moment we got the call, I knew it was from the inside and that the drama that was about to ensue was all for nothing. I remember when I first started work there. I had expected it to be different, I was trying to start fresh. Instead, I ended up getting raped into prostitution all over again.

Disguised as a legitimate massage salon, girls answer employment ads for massage therapist: no license needed. They're in tantric massage, but upon taking actual sessions, clients educate them on expectations. These are full-service brothels. Wait now john, why am I explaining this to you... You know this already. You came there often (pun intended).This is how girls are tricked into prostitution. And this is why we need Vice to shut these operations down.

How many times did you trespass on my human property? Do you know I cried while I moaned with 'pleasure'? Remember when I had run out of condoms and you forced me to do it anyway...? I laid lifeless on the massage table while your oily body slithered over me, thrusting to your climax. Wait, aren't you a cop? Was that the most appropriate place for you to be? What message do you think you were sending me? I'll tell you: not only do I get the pleasure of knowing the creepy people and the criminals of the world, but I get to know the crooked government ones too.

So anyway, you left... I stayed there, laying on that massage table, covered in your sweat and oil, sometimes crying, sometimes just in quiet shock. I felt raped. I never said no. I never stopped it. But after being sold for sex for so many years, after all the damage that had been done in all that time. After having my will and self-worth beat out of me... saying no was no longer an option for me. I wasn't allowed to stand up for myself...because I didn't know what that even meant anymore. I had no value to stand up for. All I knew in this moment was that I had been hurt and I was powerless to stop it. ...Aren't you a cop?

This is the heart of a prostitute. She can't step up, she can't get out. The only thing she's good at doing is selling her body for sex. The only thing she's WORTH doing is selling her body for sex. Yet every single time she does, she feels raped, tarnished, violated, used and discarded. That encounter with you, john, confirmed for me that there was no getting out for me. I tried... and failed.

This is why we NEED men in blue.. Except you violate that need.

One day work was unusually quiet. It was mid-morning and we all felt the uneasiness in the air, when the front desk got a call. We were going to be raided and they were about 3 minutes out. That kind of information only comes from the inside. That's when I knew everything that was about to happen was worthless and no one was in any real jeopardy. All hopes of justice were AGAIN banished.

What will it take for you to value all people equally? Or should I ask, what is it about prostitutes that makes it ok for you to participate in our exploitation? Why do you allow yourself to remain ignorant to our realities of sex trafficking?

I'm writing to all the law enforcement and government officials who were involved with my children and I back when you simply charged the man who took us with child abuse. I'm writing to every school employee, doctor, grocery store clerk, or anyone else who saw us with black and blue faces, strangulation marks on our necks, or welts on our arms. I'm writing to anyone who was concerned, but looked the other way because they didn't want to get involved.

I'm writing to every lay enforcement officer or politician who participated in our sexual services and looked the other way knowing that they were participating in our trafficked lives. I'm calling out all the men in blue whose job it is to protect and serve but instead enslave.I'm questioning the moral value of those who feel that rape-for-profit is justified as long as it has the title 'prostitution' and feel entitled to treat those women as nothing more than a human toy. Let me ask you, when you go home at night, do you set your badge down and say 'job well done'?

*****

CHAPTER 7 – CREEPY GUY

Dear john,

You have been over the top from day one. You showed up for your first appointment with roses and champagne (two of my favorites according to 'Mona's' profile on the website). Your face was beaming, smile from ear to ear, so proud of yourself and sure that you were the only one to think of such a gesture.

It was clear from the start you wanted the 'girlfriend experience'. I hated that. I preferred the one and done - you know, the in-and-out in five minutes or less guys. Those were much easier for me to handle... physically... emotionally. But you guys and your 'girlfriend experience'... the touching, the talking, the holding, the cuddling and snuggling, the kissing. You wanted intimacy. I don't have any intimacy to give you. This is a business deal... in case you missed that small detail.

In order for you to feel like there's intimacy, I have to put on a really good show... and that takes a lot of energy. It also requires me to constantly enforce boundaries, as you guys are always trying to cross them. For example, I don't kiss. Period. You can kiss my body and I'll pretend to like it. I won't kiss yours though. There will be no kissing on or around the mouth at all.

None. For whatever reason, not you or anyone else has ever been able to follow this rule. Constantly enforcing it is exhausting.

Snuggling and cuddling is usually gross because I have to smell you... and it seems to last forever. I swear time stands still. You talk about your life and I pretend to listen, as a 'psuedo-girlfriend should... but then you want me to talk. Oh god. This always amazes me. Ok, here we go...

I don't share about my personal life because you're a stranger to me. Then you say, 'but I'm a good guy. I'm not like the rest of them.' Then I lie and say 'I know, I can see that. But still... it's a safety thing.' Then you say, 'but I've shared with you all about me... you can trust me. Pleeeaaaase... I really like you and I care about you. I'm different. I want to know you.' Blah, blah...

I need to point out that you are focused on your need to be needed, not my need for privacy. There was no caring about me in this conversation. You wanted intimacy. You paid me to provide you with intimacy. You extorted intimacy. I just want to be clear about what was happening here.

So after you beg me to share details about my life, I 'give in' and tell you a pre-conceived lie that I have on hand for these kinds of situations. You're fascinated by it. Finally, with about five minutes remaining, you get your happy ending and are on your way.

I'm exhausted. I feel like you are a predator and I've just done battle for the past hour trying to keep you at bay. At the very least you are extremely needy. I'm hoping you never see me again.

No such luck, john. You see me way too much. You are quick to confess that you are falling in love with me. Honestly, I don't mind so much because all I see is dollar signs at this point. I give you my personal number and start taking advantage.

You're taking advantage of me anyway, right? Paying me for sex and companionship...? You're preying on whatever weakness I have in my life that landed me in the sex trade and you're exploiting that weakness in order to feel like a big strong virile man. I figure, why not return the favor. Your weakness is me. I can exploit that and make fast cash.

Looking back on this, I can sadly see how cold my heart had grown. I can also see that it was the only way I could survive my own life. I couldn't afford to care that you may have had feelings for me or that I may end up hurting you down the road. What's worse was I couldn't even afford to care that you were hurting me every time you touched me.

What I'm about to say may be a surprise considering you were a regular of mine for 6 very long years, but I never wanted to have sex with you. I never wanted you to touch me. I never enjoyed a single moment. Even just thinking about it made me sick, even today. I don't say that to hurt your feelings. I say that because it's the truth. I didn't choose you. Someone on the phone chose you for me. I couldn't decline; I was obligated to pay my pimp her fee once an appointment had been set, whether it actually happened or not.

By the time I gave you my number, it was my choice, I guess. But the truth, john, is that my choice was to find a way to make some money for myself and not give it all to my pimp. It had nothing to do with choosing you. You were simply a safer choice than me finding some random guy off the street. I did it to survive.

I'm hoping you can see that from my end, all of this was either a business decision or a life & death decision. Never was it a john-decision.

I'm doing better now. I'm out of the sex trade and I'm free to have the opportunity to learn what it feels like to know the love of just one man. Over time, I've been able to open my heart and I can now give (by my own free choice) the intimacy that you tried to steal from me. My heart has grown warm again.

In this thawing-out of my soul, I've begun to think of my life differently, of you differently... and I wonder why your heart was so hungry for affection. I wonder what was it that prevented you from believing that you were worthy of receiving that attention and affection freely and voluntarily from someone? Why did you feel you had to resort to paying me to be an actress - to play (or fill) the starring role in your life? Why did you feel you needed to ignore my personhood, my womanhood in order to validate your manhood?

When I finally ended my business relationship with you, it was not pretty... I was using prescription drugs and alcohol fairly heavily at this point to numb the pain and reality of the sex trade that penetrated every cell in my body and was eating me up inside. You seemed to see this as an opportunity to intrude into my life even further, which scared me. As a result, you were warned never to call or see me, in any way, ever again.

Do you remember several years later...? It was at Fred Meyer, I was cashiering. You recognized me and got really excited to see me again so you came through my line. You asked if I was still in the business and I told you very sternly 'no'. You gave me your number and asked if I'd be willing to meet with you for dinner, that you still thought about me all the time, you're finally divorced, and you still needed me. Do you remember this?

I was emotionally and physically wrecked for the rest of the day and several days thereafter. I felt like my past was in my present. Every single time I had sex with you for money was played over and over in my head. This new, clean, honest life I had been trying to build for myself just vanished because of your selfishness. You had to pick my line... you couldn't just leave me alone.

After much consideration regarding your dinner request, I decided to go ahead and meet with you, mainly because

I didn't want you to keep 'running into' me. I felt I needed to bring closure to this, to you. After a brief hello, I cut short the niceties by explaining that your presence in or around my life is unwarranted and unwanted. I respectfully asked that you ignore my existence, choose any other line at Fred Meyer, just don't choose mine. Please don't say hi or wave or acknowledge me in any way. I'm no longer a prostitute and I'm trying to move past that part of my life, which includes not seeing or talking to you. You, however, insisted that you were in love with me, you knew that I was in love with you, and that I would come to realize it in time. You asked me if I would be willing to start dating.

I asked you if you'd heard a word I said...? You claimed you had, but that you knew in your heart that no one can fake it like that...and you were willing to give me time to realize my feelings. I was shocked and mad. I declared you crazy and re-iterated that you needed to leave me alone, not to come through my line anymore, and if you see me anywhere else- ignore me. I left.

You continued to come through my line, john. I ended up having to quit Fred Meyer's because of you. I got stomach aches before work because I didn't know if my past would show up that day. I couldn't get out of bed because I was so traumatized from memories haunting me. I could go on...

I say all of that to say this: over the years I actually knew you, you took a lot from me... dignity, freedom, choice, self-respect, intimacy and privacy. But there's one thing that you took that you continued to take long after you were gone: my peace. Your ignorance and selfishness created such torment in my soul and my mind that every time I left my home, I was afraid of running into you... and if not you then who else like you is out there? Who's next who will recognize me and bring my past screaming back into the present moment...? I became afraid to get a job, john. I became afraid to live and enjoy my life.

Is that what you wanted for me?

Is that what you wanted from me?

*****

CHAPTER 8 – CROSSING THE LINE

Dear john,

This is a letter to the many, many of you that I've serviced over the years the have one thing in common. I don't remember very much about you specifically... to be honest, you all kind of blur together into one person in my mind. But every single one of you did the exact same thing at some point during your time with me: you crossed the line.

Every appointment started the same. You'd show up, money was exchanged, rules of engagement were reiterated. Usually (and hopefully) you'd shower real quick and then negotiations began.

It would always start off appropriate (I use that word loosely... this was, after all, a sex-for-hire situation... how 'appropriate' could it be?). But soon you would pull away from me and make the request that you already knew was off limits.

I would go over my rules again as sweetly as I could, but the dance had already begun. First you'd explain why you liked it. I agreed, I'm sure you did. Then you'd go into why you needed it.. I felt the pressure coming on. Keeping things playful, you might back off for a bit and then, taking a sharp right turn, you'd hit me with the big one: "I paid for you". And with that, you got what you wanted. If I didn't give in soon enough, you'd force it.

You see, john, your request... this thing that you HAD to have... crossed my boundaries. I set these boundaries for a reason and I'll help you understand why.

Because what you selfishly wanted, what you coerced or forced me to do, took my freedom, took my dignity, took my humanness. You caused me to feel like a child; back when I couldn't defend myself or protect myself and no one else would either. You took away my consent. How many before you and how many after you would do the same?

You see, not only was the prostitution a traumatizing situation on it's own, but it also resurrects past trauma, causing a person to re-live it all on a daily basis. My entire world now was nothing more than non-stop rape and molestation.

What's interesting to me is that you thought my being there with you was an actual career choice. But, I guess I can see how it was easy for you to push my boundaries. You had no idea that I was there solely out of survival. You didn't know how many pills I had to pop in order to just bring myself to see you that night or how many bottles I drank afterwards to erase the memory of what we did.

So, I'm in this bind... all I want is to be done, but in order to be done, you need to do this thing. I knew you'd get your way, john. So, I begin to disappear…

While I move into position, and you get excited, I get my "turned on" character ready. In my head, though, I drift away. It starts. I am barely aware I'm even in the room. I can't hear you, I can't hear myself, I've completely disconnected from everything. I keep drifting further and further and further away. Nothing but peace fills my mind.

The next thing I know, I'm waking up to my cell phone ringing. It's my pimp either wanting to know why I haven't left yet or if I'm ready for the next appointment. I look over at the clock. Two hours had passed since I last looked at it, which was right when you had just began.

So, apparently, you finished, took another shower (I hope) and left. I assume I had said good bye because when I saw you the next time, you never said anything about me being asleep. Then, after you left, I must have laid down and fallen asleep.

This is really very serious, john. I was so traumatized that I worked myself into amnesia. Not only is this scary, it's dangerous. What if I had gotten into my car to drive home? What if I had just started walking around the city?

I realize you didn't know what was happening, but I'm writing this letter now so that you can understand... and maybe you'll think twice before buying sex in the future. I'm the majority, not the exception. Most girls, most women in the sex trade have very unfortunate histories prior to winding up there.

Most of us were tricked, coerced, or forced into some form of prostitution when we first started... and then we either didn't know how to get out... or we were too ashamed to try.

Every single one of us has had a traumatizing experience IN the sex trade and most of us have had prior sexual trauma before the sex trade. Every time we meet with you, we are being re-traumatized. Every single time.

I realize that you may not have known any of this before... but I do know you've thought about things like this. I know this because you all have a mother. Some of you have a wife or girlfriend. Some of you have children - a daughter or even a son. Or nieces and nephews. You look out for these women and children in your lives. You are aware of danger and protect them from predators. You want happiness, goodness, and prosperity for them and you work very hard to give them that and make sure they know they're loved and feel secure.

You would be devastated if you found out that your mother was a hooker.

You would feel dirty and betrayed if you knew that your wife or girlfriend had been a prostitute prior to knowing you.

You would feel like a failure if you learned your daughter was a sex slave.

Now think of the last girl you purchased... or think of me. I'm someone's mother. I will be someone's wife. I'm also someone's daughter.

We are people too. Every hooker, every stripper, every prostitute. We belong to someone - in a good way. Someone loves us, somewhere. Someone is missing us. Someone is hurting for us. Someone is trying to help us.

You cross the line so you can enjoy your favorite thing. I disappear into the shadows of my mind just to survive my time with you, just to survive one more day so that maybe I might find my life again.

I know what your favorite thing is. You want to know mine?

My favorite thing is to be free.

CHAPTER 9 – PRICE OF LONELINESS

Dear john,

Gosh, how long were you a client of mine... five years? I'll never forget that first appointment, I was working for Her out of an in-call apartment Downtown. It was the middle of the afternoon, typical drizzly northwest weather, you were looking for a warm body to make you feel alive that day.

I welcomed you into the luxurious apartment, which was located right in the heart of the city's tourist attractions; a very public location for such secret and discrete activity. You knew me as 'Mona'. If I hadn't known better, I would have sworn you hadn't seen a woman in twenty years, you were so eager and intense. Within five minutes you had stripped down to your underwear and were tugging at mine.

You wanted passion so I played along. That was my job: to give you what you wanted, to make your fantasies become a reality. I had become very good at my job.. So good, in fact, that it was over in another five minutes. You were blown away. You had never experienced anything like that in your life. Ok.

I smiled and continued to carry on the facade that it was just as significant for me, etc... In my head, however, I was counting down - only ten minutes down... fifty still left to go, oh god What were we going to do for 50 minutes? I charge extra to go for 'round two', and I doubted you were the type who would be keen on spending that kind of cash.

So, I listened to you talk... for 45 minutes, and pretended to be interested and sympathetic to your troubles. You told me how your marriage had grown cold, your teenagers would rather gouge out their own eyes than spend time with you, they disrespect your rules... your boss refuses to acknowledge the hard work you put in, you haven't received the raise you've been promised... you felt invisible in your own life, a shadow of a man, benched for the remainder of the game.

For the first time in a very long time, with me, you felt visible again. You felt seen.

Now, suddenly, I was listening. Until that moment, I hadn't seen you. You were just another 'john'. Just another hour wasted of my life. Just a couple easy fresh hundreds in my back pocket, which for me meant one more day I could stay safe. But you felt seen and I wondered why, with me - a prostitute - of all people, you would.

I had been working in the sex trade for 3-4 years by this time and had mostly terrifying experiences that to this day traumatize me. The ones that didn't simply reminded me of the ones that did. You were the first one to make me wonder WHY all of you men were coming to me in the first place.

Fifty minutes. Time was up. Thank god. You said you'd come back. Fine.

You did, every week, like clockwork. You got your 'passion' and then your 'talk-time' and I listened to your stories about home and work. Eventually, I gave you my personal number because I got tired of giving my pimp part of the fee which allowed me to lower your hourly rate. You felt you were getting a deal, so you saw me more frequently and for longer periods of time.

You had me come to your office; I hosted you in my home. We met in strange places. You said you were falling in love with me. You wanted to be with me - not 'Mona'. The arrangement had gone too far and I terminated communication. I eventually terminated 'Mona'.

Many months later, in an effort to leave to my pimp and the sex trade altogether, I joined a church handbell choir and man, was I surprised to see you sitting in one of the pews on Sunday morning! What's more, was that you had the nerve to come and talk to me. In the months that followed, you found every excuse to be near me, talk to me, or see me at church.

Interestingly, I visited a few churches that summer to do a guest handbell performance and I ran into a handful of clients, each at a different church; very awkward. Disheartened, I left the church and the choir... ashamed and disappointed in myself, you and men in general, and God.

I went back to 'work' as 'Vivienne' for another madam and, not surprisingly, you found me there too. A short time later, her operation was busted by vice and I went to work for myself as 'Anna'. You found me as her too. Enough time had passed and you assured me that you were over me, that you just wanted the business end of the relationship. I set clear boundaries with you and we tried again.

I should have known better. You were still lonely, still starved for affection at home. You said that touching your wife was like touching ice. I bluntly told you I was faking everything with you... every single time. I wasn't actually trying to hurt your feelings, but I was trying to jolt you into the reality of our relationship: it always had been and will continue to be business-only. You didn't care. It felt real to you... and even if I was faking, at least I cared enough to fake it.

john, your obvious loneliness was the one thing that kept me from cutting you off sooner. Your loneliness is what makes me think of you every now and then even today. Not that I ever want to see you again... ever. But I wonder, how lonely does a man have to be to completely depersonalize another human being? More than that, though, I wonder how did your heart get so lonely in the first place and what can be done to actually fix that problem rather than you selfishly choosing to purchase time with me, violating my boundaries, raping me emotionally...?

Every session you had with me, you needed to have your needs filled so badly that it never once occurred to you that you PURCHASED me, that you reduced my total personal value to a few hundred bucks... you never considered how inhumane that was. Your loneliness was so severe that it made you blind.

Not once did you consider how desperate or lonely I must have been to even be in that situation, that I would have to sell my body to random strange smelly men rather than be in a beautiful relationship with a man who loves me. Never did you take into account how many men I had been with prior to you that day, or how many I would need to be with after you, and how tired, used, dirty, and traumatized my poor body was nor did you see the vacancy residing in my soul.

You have a daughter, John. How would you feel if you found out your daughter was selling herself for sex? How would you feel about the men who were paying her? I'm someone's daughter too. How do you think my dad would feel if he knew? How would he feel about you?

*****

CHAPTER 10 – WHAT DID YOU DO?

Dear john,

You knew yet did nothing. You had discovered his secrets and you saw his motives, but you stood on the sidelines like a spectator watching the tragedy unfold. So how do I categorize your level of responsibility in the kidnapping of me and my kids? Do you have a role in my eleven years of slavery? What was your contribution to our experience in the world of human trafficking?

I guess that depends on your role in our lives at the time it all started. That is the key to all of this right there, isn't it, john?

I think we'd both acknowledge at this point, that our relationship had long been over for reasons we'll set aside, but of which there was no rebounding. Our connection and living arrangement was strictly platonic, the goal being for you to find work and a place of your own. At least that's what we agreed.

You, however, were on a whole other page that included a strategy to win me back. You exploited my need for childcare as a way to continue living in my home.

Somehow, you managed to avoid getting hired –
anywhere. When I got you a job where I worked (in an
effort to get you moving), you instead interpreted that as
a sign of affection.

But things quickly took a turn south. You heard rumors
that I was dating someone at work. Even though I denied
them, you called me a liar. One night I didn't come
home at all until morning. You were furious with
jealousy and demanded an explanation. Can I tell you
something, john? I was so petrified and confused about
the events that prevented me from coming home, I
couldn't even put two thoughts together. That's why I
went in my room and shut the door without saying a
word. And it hurt me that you didn't know me well
enough to know when something was wrong. After all
the years and things we'd been through.

You didn't know this, but I was being abused and
threatened and put in very dangerous situations and I
didn't know how to handle it. Your selfishness made
things worse. I find it ironic that people claim to love
someone, but only worry about themselves. What if we
actually focused on the person that we claim to love?
How much safer would the world be?

Anyway, pressure got intense for me as my situation got
worse and my patience with you began to fade. Of
course, the more distant I got, the more angry and bitter
you became until suddenly, as if all in one huge
whirlwind, everything came to the ultimate climax.

I got dropped a bombshell of information at lunch, one day, about my very dangerous co-worker, he got fired, you had JUST moved out, he FORCED his way in, I endured beatings, you merely left paperwork in front of my house about the dangerous man who already had possession of my family. You knew he was there. You knew he was a registered sex offender for offenses against a minor. You knew my six year old son and seven year old daughter were being held by him. You knew that his last victim's children were two young boys that he had handcuffed to a railing that he had beat until they vomited.

What did you do?

What did you do to protect my children? What did you think he would do to them? Did you even care? How did you try to protect me? Did you honestly think we were safe? Why did you drop the paperwork at my house?

You claimed to love me, john. You claimed to love my children like they were your own. What did you do to protect the ones you say you loved?

Did you call the police? No. Did you come over to the house to visit? Try to possibly intervene? No. Did you tell my mom or family at least so that they could take action? No.

Why?

My children and I needed a hero. We needed someone to step up and say 'I see something that's not right'. All you had to do was make a call. That's all it takes to change or save someone's life. It would have saved mine. It would have saved my kids'. It's not about anything else. Did your jealousy paralyze you from moral obligation on behalf of humanity? I have serviced many men over my time in the sex trade… The reason they have disregard for me is because they see me as a human toy – an object for purchase…

What's the reason for yours?

*****

CHAPTER 11 – MY BOYFRIEND OR MY PIMP

Dear john,

Funny how sometimes things come around again. I was making a legit effort to try and get out of 'the life' and you and I crossed paths. It had been about a decade since we'd last seen each other since you lived with me just before my kids and I were kidnapped; when you didn't bother to do anything. But time had passed now, you apologized and I told you the result of your poor decision back then: I had been in the sex trade for the past 10 years. I thought it was nice to catch up with an old friend, but you wanted more.

Of course you were in a tight situation financially and within days you came to stay with me and shortly thereafter you wanted us to be a couple again. I'll be honest john, every aspect of that idea sent me into a dark place. I know I looked happy about it on the outside… but I had learned how to be a good actress. The truth was that I didn't want a relationship and I definitely did not want to have sex… with you or anybody else.

I was trying to get 'out of the life' which was very hard to do. I had tried a few times before, but experienced retaliation. I needed an ally. You were my best shot, so I went with the flow. But things moved so fast. Too fast. Before I knew it, it was a week before the wedding and I was trying to back out. You remember? You and my family spent an entire day convincing me not to back out and why I needed to get married. I was so distressed the day of the wedding, I had to be drunk and high just to walk down the aisle. To this day I don't remember any of it.

As I sobered up that honeymoon night, I had to be honest. "I want an annulment". I confessed I never had any feelings for you, not to take it personal but I just wasn't the same person anymore. I expressed that I did not want to be married and couldn't remain involved with you. I apologized for letting it go so far. But there was nothing I could do. That was it for me. Not for you, though. You insisted that I'd come around, so you refused to give me an annulment. Since we had already signed a lease, we ended up living together as roommates for the next two years while you waited for me to come around and I waited for you to give me a divorce.

I was working hard and it was taking a terrible toll on my body, I'd get very thin and ill for long periods making me weak. Your employment was inconsistent at best. Paying bills was getting tight. It was all falling on my head. I worked double shifts and started an at-home business as a way to try and take care of myself... my whole goal was to get out from under you (we'd been there before, this was all too familiar).

The rent came due, we couldn't make it… payment arrangements. Next month, same thing. Following month, payment arrangement – MISSED. "Pay Rent Or Vacate". Somehow over these months you worked less and less and less.

I had been TRYING to get OUT of the life. Since I met you, I got stuck further IN. I did the unthinkable: I sold myself to make sure rent got paid. You wanted to know how I did that. I was honest, I told you. So, what happened next?

Did you feel terrible and go find work? No. You sat back, very comfortable in the driver's seat as you drove me to and from jobs to pay for your bills, your rent, your electricity, your phone. You sat down in the car and waited while I was up in some unknown hotel room with one or two or three guys having who-knows-what done to me. Then I'd come down and get in the car, sore and exploited, while you joyfully drove home.

So I don't want to belabor this issue… I really just want to make sure I'm understanding this correctly. While you've been claiming to love me and 'waiting' for the love of your life' for two years, just like that, you turn around in a heartbeat, sell her body, and become her pimp?

CHAPTER 12 – THE RING

Dear john,

Actually, to be more accurate, I should say 'dear sir or madam' being as half the time the person selling me was a woman.You men can be rough, but mostly you are all about business, your bitches (or ho's) and your money. You lady pimps (madams), on the other hand, can get downright ugly. This letter is addressed to all of you who made a profit by selling my body (for sex or labor), with or without my knowledge or consent.

To my very first pimp in Vegas who I never actually knew. I had just heard stories about you and had been given the long list of do's and don'ts… and the 'or else's'. After the horrific situation I had just escaped from and continued to run from, I knew better than to call your bluff. I really only have one question for you: were you aware that no one told me I was supposed to have sex with your client? I was sent to be raped for a measly $700, ALL of which was yours. You had never met me yet you had already determined my worth. How do you do that? Is there a pie chart you look at or do you just take a wild guess? I suppose I'm supposed to say thank you, after all, you made me a prostitute, a whore, a hooker, a call girl. You started my 'career', albeit without my knowledge or consent.

To all of the 'johns' who used romance as a lure to lower my guard, making me believe I was in love and worse, that I was actually loved in return. My desperation to be chosen was used as a weapon against me, I was vulnerable in the worst way. In a sense, I was much like a child in this regard. You preyed on this hunger and drove me deeper into the vice grips of the devil himself all while I thought I was being rescued until you dropped the illusion and I fell into the bottomless pit of emotional rape and mental torture that is prostitution.

Addressing every agency and massage parlor, you realize that no matter how you package it, you are nothing more than a glorified Goodwill store? All your items have been well worn. They're over priced and then discounted. They're unwanted and discarded... over and over and over. How is it that you can't see that the women you sell are women just like YOU? Can you imagine having sex with twelve different strangers in one day? Or being sent on 'tour' to a strange city somewhere across the country for a week, never being able to leave your hotel room because you have a client on the hour every hour from 9:00am until 1:00am? That's fifteen clients a day for five or six days straight.

Last but not least, my favorite group of 'johns': the reviewers. I just want to say thank you for giving me a human Yelp review of my forced, enslaved performance with you. Thank you for the ratings and additional comments that made me feel like an irrelevant non-person. I felt like a steak being graded. I have few words for the degradation you subjected all of us to by your review boards and sites. I'll just say that I'm thankful that I've found my value now, you did NOT steal that from me.

To all of you above, I call you The Ring as you all contribute to each other, working together to keep this thing called trafficking, this illusion of prostitution going. Each of you having a certain 'role' to play and let me just say that we understand how this goes. But that's not what I want to talk about right now.

What I want to say to all of you, as you each play your part in this thing called trafficking, is are you aware, or do you even care, the damage you do to a person when you put a price tag on their forehead? Every time you sell someone at any fee, that's a price tag and we live with that. It does something to a person.

It's like taking a twenty dollar bill and consistently selling over and over for only twenty cents. How does the twenty dollars know it's worth twenty dollars anymore when people keep buying for only twenty cents? You put that price tag of twenty cents on the twenty dollar bill. It's YOUR responsibility that the self-perceived value dropped. It's YOUR responsibility that the twenty dollar bill doesn't know who or what it is anymore. Whose responsibility is it to fix that? Who will take the price tag off?

And when you sell a person to another person, you have put a label on our back that say "property of….." and some of you actually brand us with tattoos or burns MAKING us your property. My first trafficker did. Can you imagine what it's like to be someone's personal property? It's like not knowing how to think for yourself because you're not allowed to. It's like not being able to have feelings or have any needs. You can't say no or tell someone to stop because you're not your own person anymore… you're someone else's.

When you place an ad for me, you're literally placing an ad for ME, for someone to buy me. They do what they want with me. You think I can set boundaries? No. Clients don't respect boundaries. What you've done, is you made me a human toy. I have to do what they want, how they want, when they want, they way they want, for how long they want until they're done with me and toss me aside. And I'm to wait until someone wants to 'play' with me again.

It would appear that each you operate unique and individual, but you're not.You all do the same thing and we are your target. The same rules apply, nothing changes All of you are traffickers and exploitation is your game. Fear is your tool. You may use violence. Perhaps you threaten our family or blackmail some aspect of our lives. Maybe you exploit our need for money and entrap us in the life. Somehow you get us in and once we're in you don't let us leave. Fear. Fear of retaliation. Some of us experience it. I do – three times. Others only hear about it. It's so severe, the fear is enough to keep you from leaving.

Package it the way you like. There's a name for all of you, john. It's called 'the Ring'.

CHAPTER 13 – MR. ED

Dear john,

I don't remember your name, but I remember you went by Mr Ed in your email. You were a much older gentleman and lived very far away in a small town in central WA, which was a 3.5 hour drive each way for me. I was 'Anna' at the time and took you on as a client because I knew I could use your distance to my advantage financially.

As I approached your home for the first time, I grew increasingly nervous, realizing just how in-the-middle-of-nowhere I was. If you were to do something to me, no one would ever know. You lived on a lot of land that included a farm with a river running through the back. I liked the river. I found myself going back to the river often in my mind during my service to you.

My total fee was $1400: travel fees to and from plus a four hour session to include my giving you a bath, giving a massage, receiving a massage, and a happy ending for you. I had been clear on the phone that this did not include full service (sexual intercourse); that would increase the fee.

What I couldn't explain to you then, but I can now is that by the time you became my client, I had been a 'working girl' for nearly a decade. That's a lot of wear-and-tear on a person and I was tired. Being as I was not working for a pimp anymore, I could write my own rules, and for many of my clients, I chose to only do sensual massage (happy ending included) rather than full service because to be honest, I just couldn't handle having sex anymore. It got to the point where I didn't think I physically could do it. I had even gotten really good at 'accidentally' stimulating a premature ending to save myself.

But, boy, you really wanted full service... and I did everything I could to deter you by raising my fee so high, I was hoping you wouldn't pay. You almost did.

We started with the bath - you alone in the tub (your choice) as I bathed you for nearly an hour. I found that odd, quite frankly. You looked uncomfortable and clearly didn't fit; standing 6'6" tall with quite a round mid-section. It was a normal clawfoot tub. You were looking for romance, wanting my sweet smiles and sparkles in my eyes. Cynically, I was thinking you were not in touch with reality. I was sure to keep my face hidden from you, but pulled out my softest sing-song voice to appease your delusion. Once you were relaxed, you began to dwell on your troubled marriage... how you wish you could leave your wife, but you would loose all your money, she's that kind of woman. Your first wife was the love of your life, but she died. You knew you'd never love like that again, so you settled for this woman and she is sucking your life and your money dry. It was during this dissertation I first found reprieve in my head by the river.

Before I knew it, bath-time was over and we moved into the bedroom; time for my massage. You were very excited to be able to give me this gift... you and everyone else who thinks they're the only one who offers to touch me. I would like to tell you something... I didn't want to be touched by you. I didn't want to be touched by anyone. Especially all of you who were paying me to touch me. You all had destroyed touching for me, made it ruthless and evil. Not surprisingly, during your massage, I made my second mental escape to the river.

The hour passed quickly (due to what I now understand as dissociation - a tool commonly used during trauma). My escapes to the river were complete disconnects from what was going on with you because I had reached maximum mental capacity. You assumed position to receive your massage, I went on auto-pilot and back to the river.

At some point, I gave you your 'pop' a little early, so we 'cuddled' for the remainder of your time. I had so much anxiety, Mr Ed. I couldn't wait to leave.

Finally, you got up and I couldn't get out of there fast enough. I felt so gross, I could smell you on me all the way home... it was a very long drive. I don't remember much of the drive, I know I got lost a few times because of that and what I do remember involved massive tears. $1400 didn't seem worth all that I was dealing with.

But I saw you a few more times, 6-8 weeks in between visits, which gave me some time to recover from the last. Each time, though, you would pressure me for full service and you were now prepared and willing to pay the additional $500 for said service. I started coming up with excuses as to why I couldn't.

Finally one day I found myself in a situation where I needed money fast. I was trying to, once again, transition to a 'legit' life but ironically that requires money. I gave in and for a flat $2K, agreed to 4.5 hours and full service at the end.

Mr. Ed, I understand that you were completely in love with your first wife and how crushed your heart must have been at losing her so early in life. I understand that loneliness caused you to settle for a second wife that leaves you starving for affection and full of regrets. I can appreciate all your pain. Your pain, however, caused you to contact me and purchase me, caused you to push me and pressure me. Here is what I did the day after I agreed to provide you with full service:

I consumed 5 Xanax upon leaving your house in order to stop shaking just to get myself home. I got home at 4am and consumed a bottle of red wine and 10 more Xanax. Drunk and high, I drove to Starbucks for coffee, got cigarettes, and sat outside long enough to smoke through 1 1/2 packs while I replayed what you did with me the night before over and over and over. I went inside and took the rest of my Xanax and a lethal combination of several other prescription drugs that I had. Then I went to my booze stash and swallowed everything.

While I was waiting for death to consume me, I went to find my razor blades. I began to make jagged incisions in random places on my body: my face, my chest, my leg, my stomach. All those places that men think are sexy...that you think are sexy... they were tarnished, mutilated, ruined. Only no one could see the damage - silent wreckage. In my death, I would be sure to give my devastation a voice.

So we're clear, Mr Ed, the day after I last saw you, I attempted to take my life.

Your pain caused my pain... and my pain almost ended my life.

In short, Mr Ed, your overwhelming loneliness nearly cost me my life.
.

I have a problem with this. I'm sure you let yourself off the hook easy because the choice to see you from the very beginning was mine. I could have said no at any time. In your eyes, you hold no responsibility what-so-ever. I would like to help you connect the dots and clear up any confusion you may have about prostitutes who are trapped working for a violent pimp who takes all her money versus a private independent prostitute who places her ads herself and keeps all her cash. I would like to help you see that your loneliness is your responsibility... to be dealt with in a healthy way, a way that doesn't violate the soul of another human being.

First of all, most independent girls started by accident because someone exploited and took advantage of a young and trusting heart which turned into a pimp/prostitute relationship. For several reasons, much like with a gang, its very difficult (and dangerous) to get out once you're in.

The more 'seasoned' (used) she becomes, the smarter she operates and if she can keep her nose fairly clean, she eventually can get free. However, by that time, her entire person is changed. Her will has been broken, her view of the world forever tarnished because she's the dark, dirty secret behind every successful business man, government official, married man, father, and otherwise up-standing citizen. She's become dead inside and emotionless in order to perform the 'job' and acquired a whole new skill set for this lifestyle. Re-joining regular, everyday life is traumatic and foreign, not to mention that working for minimum wage doesn't even make sense now. Why would she work for a week just to make what she could easily make in an hour?   So she does what she does best, the only thing she knows how to do in order to survive: she pimps herself out.

In no way in this a choice. No girl, no woman is faced with an opportunity to choose to be a flight attendant and travel, let's say, or choose to have sex with a strange fat smelly man and says "I choose the latter." It's not about 'choice'. It's about survival.

I did NOT choose you. I was trying to choose to never ever have to service another man. I was trying to get free... trying to buy my way out.

You felt I had a choice. The truth is that I was trapped in a lifestyle... so trapped that I thought that death was the only way out.

Because of your indifference to my boundaries as a person, or even as a prostitute... because of your relentless, self-centered pursuit of my soul... because you reduced me to an item of possession that you could own for those four hours... and mainly because you refused to actually deal with the emptiness in your heart and talk with your wife...

...because of all that, your pain nearly cost me my life... and had I not lived, I wouldn't have found the person that was still living deep down inside me. I wouldn't have been able to hold the broken pieces of my heart in my own two hands, embracing my wounds, celebrating each little victory - one by one - that makes my heart whole again. Had I not lived, I would never have been able to look in the minor and seen how strong, beautiful and unique I really am... full of life and ready to shine! I wouldn't have realized that I'm not everyone's dark dirty little secret, but rather an Ambassador of Hope, Freedom, and Survivorship!

Mr Ed, I survived your pain... I survived mine... and I know that one day there will be a man who doesn't treat me like the prostitute I used to be, but instead like the lady I've always been.

CHAPTER 14 – PRINCE CHARMING

Dear john,

You were the most beautiful man I'd ever seen. After having spent 11 years in 'the life', I didn't think I wanted a relationship until you showed up and changed everything. It was a fairytale from the beginning, you stole my heart, a fast and furious romance. I was sure this was the real thing or so I told myself. I had been free for two years and was ready to finally have a purpose. I decided you were my purpose and that was the most dangerous thing I had ever done.

Within months, you put a ring on my finger, I nearly fainted at the sight, scared to wear something so valuable. We had big plans and part of them included my finishing this book. We would go to fancy dinners and celebrated beautiful anniversaries. Every time we went out it was intimate and special. We made memories.

We made a home together and we loved to cook together. Our walls and shelves were covered with our pictures. We had a long playlist of songs that we 'our songs' and we loved to dance. We never watched a movie and didn't even own a TV. We talked. You traveled a lot and that was really rough on me.

Sometimes you were gone for several weeks at a time, but we'd always make a big deal about it when you came home. This was our life and I love it.

But several months later, I became unable to write. Tragedy Devastation hit me like a tidal wave. Betrayal in its worst form. It was in this moment I realized I was a fly trapped in a spider's web.

You had been working me from the start. I told you on day one that I was a survivor; your tentacles began to wrap around me, but I failed to notice...love struck. I proudly had two years under my belt, but only two years... I was whole enough to see red flags, too raw still to guard against attacks. You preyed on my vulnerabilities, you groomed me like all the pros. You abused me in the most subtle ways. You isolated me from all my family and friends. I stopped all my hobbies. My whole world revolved around your next text and, if I was lucky, your phone call.

Being your wife became the reason I had survived my life of trafficking. If I wasn't your wife, then why was I alive?

You created that... and you knew I wouldn't leave. I didn't. The abuse got worse. Emotional and mental games got so intense that I resorted to self harm. I wanted to die.

How can you do that to a person? Knowing what I had been though? What is the matter with you? You kept blaming me, telling me it was all in my head, that I was creating problem. You told me things were my fault. You made me feel like I was crazy. But I wasn't crazy, john, you created this whole mess.

Over a year later, while continuing therapy, one day I my therapist said to me "Julia, you know you're backsliding." Yes, I did. And john, I spent that entire weekend writing down every red flag since I first met you. I connected the dots that I already knew. When I figured it out, I realized I knew it the whole time What petrifying is that I came so close to falling victim to the same life I just escaped. But I had healed enough to stop it.I was strong enough to stand up for myself. When I realized what you were trying to do to me, I wasn't scared... I was angry. Do you know what happened next?

I terminated everything the next day. I got strong that day. I rediscovered my intuition and my boundaries that day. I learned to trust MYSELF that day. I learned not to place my purpose in a person.

And after that, I picked up my book and started to write.

*****

CHAPTER 15 – CINDERELLA

Dear Friend,

My heart is like yours. It trusts. It loves. It's been broken. It's been picked up and put back together. We all experience love differently. It's scary to give it, it's hard to receive.

We all want to be seen, valued, protected, heard. We want to be honored. We want to be chosen. None of us wants to get left behind.

We've done (and will do) many things to fit in, to be successful,to avoid rejection.

In our relationships, they'll pursue us, adore us, romance us, cherish us. Some will hurt us, leave us, forget us.

Let me say this to you: YOU determine your worth, no one else. CHOOSE your passion, don't wait on someone else's, There is no relationship worth sacrificing your integrity, but how can you know if that's what's happening? KNOW who you are. Take the TIME to discover your interests and hobbies. FIND your friends, the real ones. VALUE their feedback and give them yours. If it doesn't feel right, then it's not right. PERIOD. You're never wrong.

No one defines you. You're not less, you're not more. No one makes you. YOU make you.

You don't need to be rescued. You can change your life. What's your DREAM? I don''t care where you are in life. What's your dream? Why am I asking? Because you have to know where you're going in order to get there. And NOBODY else can tell you where that is. YOU decide your value. YOU decide your worth. You're accepted because YOU say so.

Do we want certain things? Yes. Should we sacrifice the core of who we are for it? NO. You are who you say you are.

I got out of 'the life' by myself. I almost died , twice, trying to do it. After being out for two years, I met a man and put my future in his hands. I told myself he was going to take care of me financially. He was going to give me a house. He was going to give me the love I so desperately wanted and needed. ALL my eggs were in one basket.

Survivors struggle. I had been struggling in every way. My finances were in bad shape. I had just been fired, that was the fourth or fifth job I had either lost or quit in two years. I didn't know where I was going to go from there. I was barely making it. For much of those two years, I barely had food. Sometimes, not even a home. I didn't want to be struggling anymore. I needed life to get easier. It had been hard for way too long.

Then 'he' came along. My Prince Charming. I believed in him because I needed to. I believed in him for all the wrong reasons. I felt like his love redeemed me from all the tarnished years before. I felt chosen instead of thrown away. I thought I needed a him in order to make me valuable again. But, when I found out the truth, I discovered who I am. And that's when I realized you don't need a Prince Charming in order to be a Cinderella.

###

*****

AFTERWORD

Thank you for ready my book, I hope it touched you in a unique way. My writing started while I was still enslaved, however I had focus and direction with this project once I finally was free. My anniversary date is February 1, 2012. It took four years to write this book... And in saying that, you'd think there'd be more here. But this was such a difficult piece to write. Each letter went through five or six phases before it became presentable and something I would be willing to offer to you as the reader and that would portray the correct emotion without unnecessary rage or offensive language.

I've grown significantly through this process, something many survivors don't have the opportunity to do. The wounds are real. This crisis is in your backyard. We don't all need to join a campaign, but we do all need to participate in prevention.

I survived... But I live with permanent physical and mental disorders that prevent me from living a normal, as-per-usual life. Myself and so many other survivors fight every day to help fix and prevent this from happening, we've made advocacy in the anti-trafficking movement our career... We do it for you.

I'm excited to release me next book which will be the actual memoir of my life, including my mental illness and how that played out during my time in slavery. Keep your eye out for 'Shatter Me'. You can follow my writing at juliaandersonwriter.wordpress.com

BIOGRAPHY

Being a survivor of human trafficking, Julia Anderson has seen the darkest of evils, spending years intimately involved with societies' deepest secrets. "I know what no one wants to know." She believes she survived eleven years of slavery to share her story and let it be used in many different platforms to aid efforts to stop human trafficking, assisting to make awareness a national priority.

Though raised in an affluent family, Julia's struggles started early in life with an abusive childhood. She went on to become a mother at age 17 and a flight attendant, followed by her years as a trafficked victim.

Repeat trauma over the course of her thirty-plus years has resulted in severe PTSD, which is a silent but very real disability.

Today, Ms. Anderson relies on her psychiatric service dog, Allie, who helps her manage that along with other physical and mental residual ailments from her 'time in'. She feels mental illness is an overlooked issue strongly connected to trafficking.

Julia admires Steve Jobs and quotes him as saying "The very nature of people is something to be overcome." She couldn't agree more. She believes that each moment happens only once, time is priceless yet the most overlooked and wasted gift. She's a very passionate person and the most happy when she's freely pursuing life, moment to moment.

Speaking and writing are her gifts. Sharing her story by doing what she loves makes surviving worth it. Julia lives in Seattle, Wa and owns Touch One Lose None where she writes and conducts counterintuitive human trafficking training. touchonelosenone.com

"Many people are guarded because they've been HURT. Trafficked victims and survivors are guarded because someone PROFITED from it. " –Julia Anderson